LIGHT

SCIENCE SECRETS

Jason Cooper

The Rourke Corporation, Inc.
Vero Beach, Florida 32964

Edited by Sandra A. Robinson

PHOTO CREDITS

© Lynn M. Stone: cover, title page, pages 4, 8, 12, 13, 18, 21; courtesy NASA, pages 7, 17; courtesy Edison/Ford Winter Estates, page 10; courtesy Sharplan Lasers, Inc., page 15

LIBRARY OF CONGRESS

Library of Congress Cataloging-in-Publication Data

Cooper, Jason, 1942-
Light / by Jason Cooper.
p. cm. — (Science secrets)
Includes index.
Summary: Provides a simple discussion of the sources and kinds of light, colors, and how eyes see.
ISBN 0-86593-166-6
1. Light—Juvenile literature. [1. Light.]
I. Title. II. Series: Cooper, Jason, 1942- Science secrets.
QC360.C66 1992
535—dc20 92-8808
CIP
AC

TABLE OF CONTENTS

LIGHT

On a bright day we can easily see the objects around us. Light allows us to see. When light disappears, we have **darkness.**

Light is a kind of **energy,** or power. Light comes from several places. We make some of our light, but our most important light comes from nature—the sun.

Lighting up the Chicago night

THE SUN'S LIGHT

Imagine the sun as a distant, but mighty, ball of energy producing light and heat. The sun's heat makes light which reaches 93 million miles through space to earth.

The sun's light makes "daytime." It also makes enough warmth so that we can live on most of the earth's land. Without sunlight, the earth would be too cold for living things.

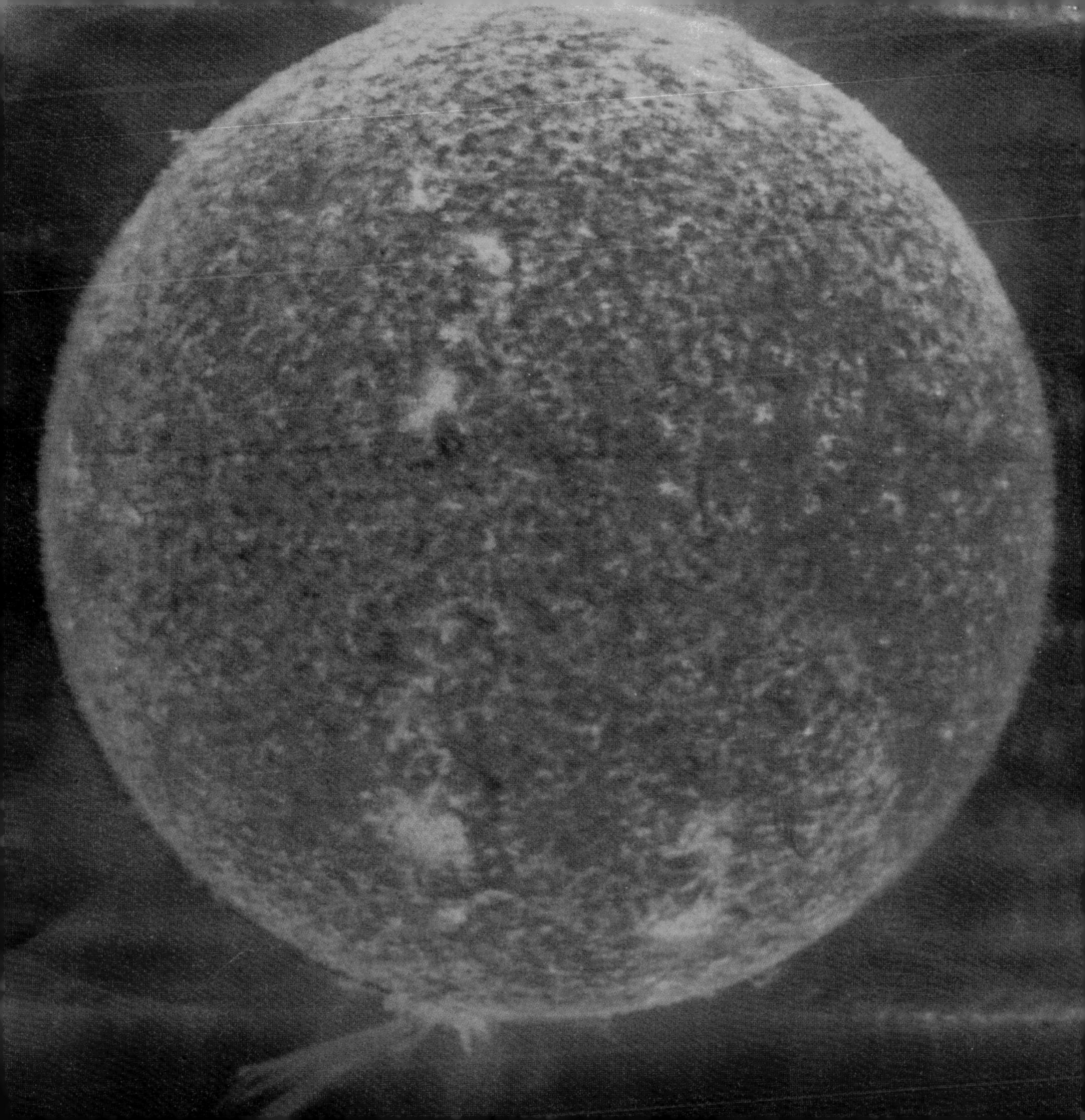

SUNLIGHT AND SUNFLOWERS

Sunlight warms our air and lights our way. But it is important for another reason. Sunlight is actually "food" for green-leafed plants. Green-leafed plants like sunflowers, trees, grass and hay, need sunlight to grow. And plants, along with the animals that eat them, are food for us! Had a hamburger lately? Thank the sun.

Plants grow in sunlight

CONTROLLED LIGHT

People want to see at night and in dark places. Open fires lit caves and camps for early humans. Later, people burned oil and gas in lamps.

In 1882 Thomas Edison, an inventor, began electric light service for a few customers in New York. Today, electric lights are used throughout the world.

Inventor Thomas Edison

A modern light bulb

An Oregon lighthouse

LASERS

Laser light is a very special and powerful beam of light. Tiny bits of light energy called **photons** work together in the laser beam. (Photons also make up ordinary light, but in a different way.)

Laser light has many uses. A laser beam can cut an orange—or a steel wall.

Laser beam slices an orange

BOUNCING LIGHT

The sun is a **source** of light, a place from which light comes. Lightning and electric lights are too.

The moon, however, is bright only because the sun shines on it. Sunlight strikes the moon and bounces back—**reflects**—toward earth.

Most of the things around us reflect light rather than make light.

Moon reflects sun's light to earth

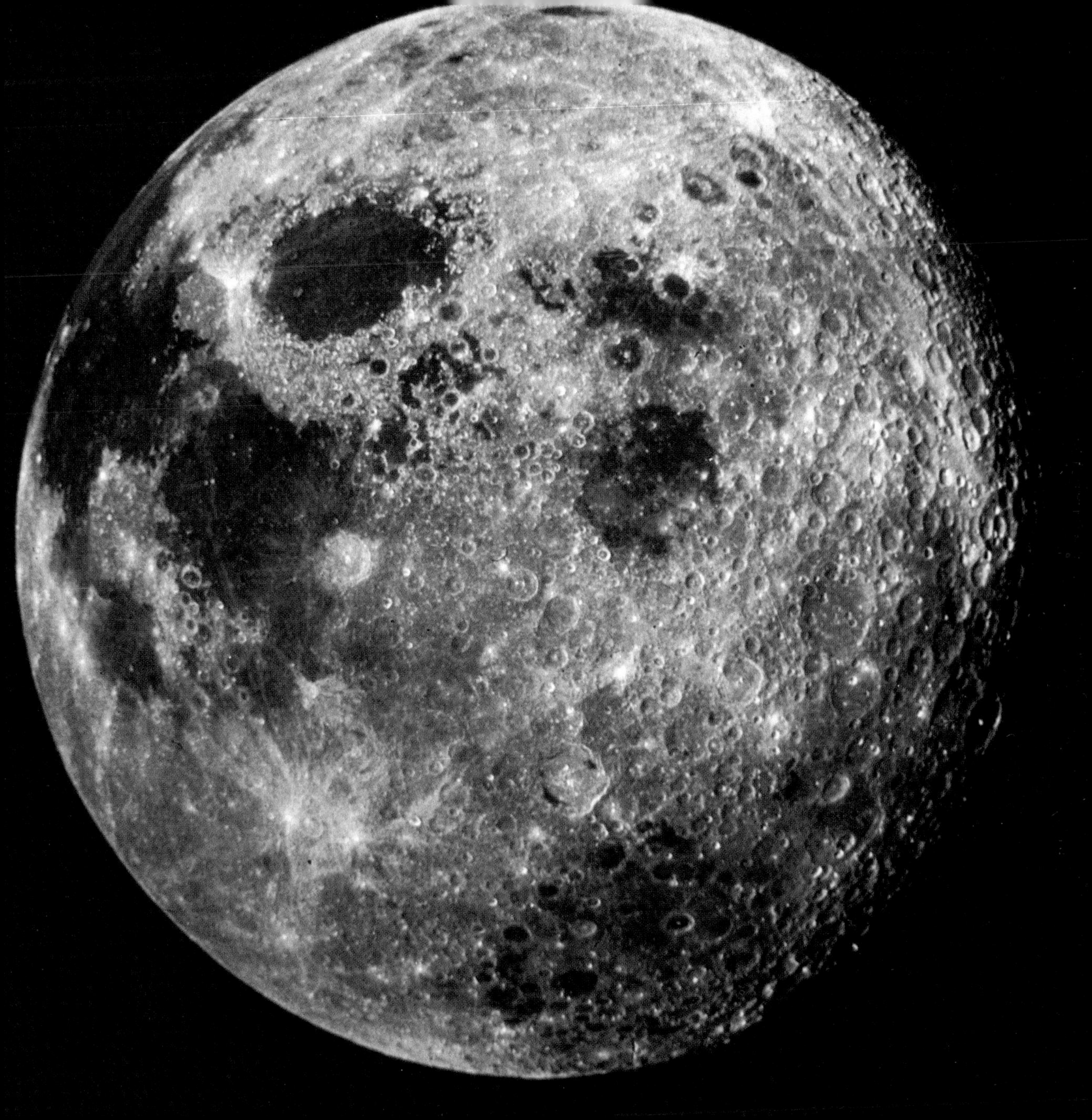

COLORS AND LIGHT

A beam of sunlight looks white, or perhaps yellow, to our eyes. But what our eyes can't see is that sunlight is really a mixture of colors.

A red flower soaks up all the colors of the sunlight that strikes it, except the red color that it reflects. Green leaves soak up all colors except green.

A red flower reflects the color red

HOW EYES SEE LIGHT

Light enters an eye through an opening called the **pupil.** Other parts of the eye react to the light and send messages to the brain. The brain makes a "picture" of what the eye sees.

Without light, a person would see nothing. Even an owl, which has excellent eyesight in dim light, cannot see in complete darkness.

Eyes send "light messages" to brain

RACING AGAINST LIGHT

You can block the path of light. You can bend light, too. Curved glass, for example, bends light and changes how things look. (They look bigger and closer, or smaller and farther away!) But you can't outrun light.

Light travels at 186,282 miles per second. Nothing moves faster. The light that the moon reflects takes less than one second to reach earth.

Glossary

darkness (DARK ness) — without light

energy (EN er gee) — power; the ability to work

laser (LAY zer) — special, powerful form of light used in medicine, communications and other fields

photon (FO ton) — a tiny, invisible bit of light energy; a bundle of light energy released by other particles (bits) called atoms

pupil (PUE pull) — the part of the eye that allows light to enter it

reflect (re FLEKT) — to bounce back, return, such as sunlight reflecting—bouncing back—from the moon

source (SORSS) — the place from which something comes

INDEX